WHITE SPACE POETRY ANTHOLOGY

WHITE SPACE
POETRY ANTHOLOGY

EDITED BY MAYA WASHINGTON

WHITE SPACE POETRY PROJECT

MINNEAPOLIS | LOS ANGELES

EST. 2010

White Space Poetry Anthology

Edited by Maya Washington

White Space Poetry Project

Running Water Entertainment, LLC

Minneapolis, MN

ISBN-13: 978-0615622873

ISBN-10: 0615622879

Editor: Maya Washington

Designer: David Oui

Cover image: Aminah Shabazz

Editorial Assistance:

Athan Bezaitis

Ian Chestnut

Hafizah Geter

Tina Simms

Printed in the United States of America

To our supporters throughout the world.

CONTENTS

11 Foreword
Maya Washington

12 White Space
Bianca Spriggs

13 On Never Speaking Again
Raymond Luczak

16 Bell
Kelli Stevens Kane

17 Reprise
Phillip B. Williams

18 The Word Snow
Su Smallen

20 Sedative
Rachel Fogarty-Oleson

22 Idiosyncratic Runes
Sandy Beach

24 Learning How to Go
Kristen Ringman

26 At the Heart of the Shipwreck
Jessica Fox-Wilson

33 You Burn Me
Haley Lasché

35 From The Twitstat Project
Renee Zepeda

39 Deaf People Worship S e x I d o l Naked - Breaking N e w s From The Washington Post
Christopher Heuer

41 Matricide
Matthew Stranach

42 Still Life with Hands, Wishes and Plate
Chiyuma Elliott

44 Zebra
Su Smallen

45 A Girl Named _____
Bianca Spriggs

47 Inside Out
Kristen Ringman

49 What of a Body
L. Lamar Wilson

50 Wild You
Matthew Stranach

52 Writing in English
Karen Christie

53 Scavenger
Zendrea Mitchell

56 Language Lesson
Ashaki M. Jackson

57 Darkness
Tara Lee Bautista

58 Chance
Autumn Joy Jimerson

60 Family Conversations
Raymond Luczak

61 It Sits on Them, Like Eggs
Keith Wilson

62 Exorcisms I Have Tried
Kimberly Eridon

64 Note from a Prodigal Son I
Randall Horton

66 Vice(s)
Daniel O. Harris

67 White Shoes
Destiny Birdsong

68 What is a Sign Language Poem?
Donna Williams

70 Self Consciousness
Kimberly Eridon

72 Me My Hearing Aids
Zendrea Mitchell

74 Revenant
Khary Jackson

75 Solace Against Emptiness
Sandy Beach

77 Dactylology
Raymond Luczak

78 The Last Morning
Sarah Roesler Conbere

80 Things I Know Like the Back of My Hands
Chiyuma Elliott

81 Zulaikha: On Falling
Bianca Spriggs

82 Given
Kelli Stevens Kane

84 Stones Formerly Known as Love
Michelle Whittaker

86 Spiral Grounding
Sandy Beach

88 Bitter/Better
Christopher Heuer

91 One Deed Another Begets
Randall Horton

92 Instead, a Tiny Metal Elephant
Rachel Fogarty-Oleson

93 The Floater
Michelle Whittaker

94 Post-Modern
Keith Wilson

96 Insertion
Curtis Robbins

100 The Dizzy Gillespie Test
Daniel O. Harris

102 It's Just That the Sun Has Bones Made of People
Hafizah Geter

103 Recurring Eargasm
Randall Horton

104 Last
Kelli Stevens Kane

107 Contributors

115 The Editor

116 White Space Poetry Project

FOREWORD

In her poem, The Word Snow, Su Smallen conjures, "Printing words brings forward dark space, brings forward what I protect." The White Space Poetry Anthology seeks to explore the darkness and light that are often the literal white space between the lines; the spaces between hearing and deaf, and the commingling inner and outer lives of the artist. In assembling this anthology, we were particularly interested in voice as it pertains to the artist's point of view: be it regional, cultural or individual perspectives. The poems herein include the work of both hearing and deaf artists. By including both Sign Language poets and those who approach their work in written English, this anthology provides an opportunity to explore visual language through linguistic "handshapes" that appear on the page. We hope that you enjoy this collection of poetry, creative non-fiction, and art, exploring white space and its literal or metaphorical presence on the page.

Maya Washington

Creative Director
White Space Poetry Project

White Space

By some trick of midnight,
the parking lot across the street
is a cold blank canvas.

I want to kiss it.

What if
        (what IF)
I climb the fence to reach it—
        lay face down—

        find

that nothing can live there.

Not an ember of breath.
Not even the memory of having
        once breathed.

And worse.

What if I find
        I cannot feel

        my lips.

Bianca Spriggs

On Never Speaking Again

for James Wright, in memoriam

1.

They say you died of cancer of the tongue.
I have had dreams of never speaking again.
My hands, bottled with the champagne of signs,
would explode and fizzle with phrases
impossible to translate into mere English.
My ears have long lost the nuances of speech.
Reading lips opening and closing is not pretty.
My eyes, closing at last, feel like a waterfall.

2.

My grandfather worked in the iron mines.
The last one closed in 1967, two years
after I was born. Everything was already dying.
It didn't matter that a fiberglass Hiawatha Indian
stood 50 feet tall with a peace offering
overlooking my hometown. Friends and neighbors
trickled out of sight. Sometimes
I had to wonder if they did exist.

3.

I walk among deaf people signing.
Their facial expressions might seem extreme,
almost grotesque to those who do not know
how to read: To become proficient
in another person's language, one must suffer.

Raymond Luczak

13

4.

I stood on the edges of collapsed mine shafts
and peered down into these cave-ins,
bowls of saplings with puddles of rusty water

at the bottom. Dreams have a way
of scaling heights whether high or low.
I saw myself coast down, a Peter Pan
darting like a quicksilver snake among the blades.
I shimmered in the evening sun.

5.

When you died, I didn't know who you were.
I was too busy writing my American Top 40 poems,
trying to be rockstar famous.
I didn't know my work was bad, amateurish.
My classmates called me a runt.
I was a lousy suicide attempt. No one even knew.

How much I needed that lie of being good
when I was still an ugly duckling.

6.

People proud of their ability to master
spoken foreign languages stumble
when it comes to hands talking volumes.
They are easily put in their places,
a bittersweet lesson like rhubarb eaten raw.

Deaf people's hands are sugar
freely borrowed in each other's measuring cups.

7.

I've scorched ants with my magnifying glass.
I've swung a dead skunk on a rope off a telephone pole hook.
I've tried to capture fireflies with a jar.

Each moment became a poem, effortless as air;
each a memory that my own family claims
never happened. No matter. I remember.

This, I've finally understood, is poetry.
Simple and ugly things are lovely in equal measure.

Sing. Silence is thundering everywhere.

Bell

these ears hear the constant tail
end of cymbals, the resonant fizz
sound waves sizzling. this
is my silence. my quiet wears zills
can't stop clapping. this body
a bell the soul rings to hear itself singing
this body a bell the soul rings
to hear itself sing.

Kelli Stevens Kane

Reprise

Across frost-
laden river,
a wolf creeps
from convex
tree trunks,
pushed from
their centers
by air given
body, shape,
bone white.
Wolf's flesh
snowed in.
Wolf now
pallid flush,
nothing, iced
body blown
inside out.
Tree, wind,
a warning: yes

Phillip B. Williams

The Word Snow

Printing words brings forward dark space, brings forward what I protect. I light my wordlessness. That long year I was capable only of referring you to "The Glass Essay." If the word is *snow*, it is not the lee of trees, not the dog lying in the road, not the architecture of cradling. If the word is *light*, it derives from snow bringing forward the world's boundlessness. The lambent amber moon, curving toward eclipse, sidelights the river birch and golden grasses. In this light I walk to the drift-carved peninsula, onto the ice-glazed sundial. I remember a girl in white with her beagle, and I am simply happy, and numb with snow.

Su Smallen

Douglas Despres

Sedative

Rachel Fogarty-Oleson

He begins and ends in silence
a single pedestrian.
I have fallen in love
with Denver
in the mountains, crisp air,
amid the crags, and valleys,
the buildings like scenery.
I wanted him to contain me.

He feels like chilled vodka slipping down
the throat. A lighter hand,
the other half of loss,
he lets me explore my roots:
whisks me away
down the tundra
—birds, fallen leaves
and small cries.

...all I wanted was
to be kissed: bent like Uri Geller's spoon—
phenomenal,
I wanted to fall, tugged by gravity.

Later, low branches; a lost ocean
his body a sun-baked stone
his mind
a kind of rush.

I crave to write his name
on dry paper,
over and over,
over
and over.

Idiosyncratic Runes

(translated glyphs)

5
leaf   bark   scree   twig root
seeking out your kind

the ones who speak

the same tongue

as your addled songlines

4
imploding   all meaning and context
  from the continuum
   of thought patterns
    rockandroll   mood   pendulum

3
dis   orderly debris
    sweet ambient dreamless sleep
        chaos–struck   morbidity

2
alphabetic   geometry
rationalized compost

1
markings

Sandy Beach

Douglas Despres

Learning How to Go

Kristen Ringman

City lights of yellow and gold,
but my eyes cannot stray
from the distant blinking of the green cans,
the winking red nuns, begging me
to let loose my dock lines, hurry
towards the channel, the lighthouses,
the harbor seals, the flocks of black and white birds
I had never known before I sailed.

What else is there now besides
the low flight of a gull, teasing
the surface of the water with its reflection,
flying fish—forgetting
their world ends where ours begins,
that rippling surface. I've always been in between—
hearing and deaf, women and men,
body and spirit, one religion and another—and now
I float between sea and land, water and air, building fires
in my hearth to keep warm through a new winter of
breaking mini glaciers around the boat, loosening
dock lines to adapt to the fall and rise of the tides.

I jump at the chance to leave
these temporary docks behind, find
other places to anchor, other moorings to steal
in the darkness. Discover continents, integrate
with locals fleetingly before the sea calls back, before
the tide turns and the sirens interrupt
the sound of the waves with songs that break hearts
or carry them away.

One day, I'll find I've grown gills, one day
my sea legs will not be fit to balance
on the hard land. Such ground is too still for my liking
already. Who ever heard of rocks that don't move? Dirt
that doesn't drift and reshape itself each day?
Aren't we more like the sea?

We humans were born against blades of grass, beneath
oak trees and birches, building houses that stay.
When the real lesson—is learning how to follow
the blinking green lights
out of the channel—learning how to go.

Jessica Fox-Wilson

At the Heart of the Shipwreck

I. At the Heart of A Shipwreck

At the heart of a shipwreck
is a child

listening to the boards   listening to her parents

groan/scream
from so much
pressure.

At the heart of a shipwreck
is a child

feeling the ship   feeling her home

tremble/rumble
from some un-
seen catastrophe.

At the heart of a shipwreck
is a child

watching the boards   watching her parents

fissure/crack
from lightning bolt fractures,
finally break apart.

At the heart of a shipwreck
is a child

staring into a hungry mouth   broken boards/splintered teeth

shiver/sink
descend into black depths,
learn to breathe water.

II. deep inside weighs

flailing
in frigid blue,
remnants of destruction
float past. she grabs what resembles
a broken piece of the ship. in the dark, everything
looks the same. instead, it's a safe, door swinging wide.
she crawls inside; she's just the right size. as she submerges,
deep inside weighs the notion that she pulled the first screw out
of the boards, just to see the ship crack open, the contents
spill out. sinking inside her black box, she finally
hits the bottom. her door opens. water
bombards her. at the bottom,
everything looks different,
blue shattered
glass.

III. Legacy of His Disappearance

Without mother without father without fully

stocked, equipped ship, I am trying

to rebuild my old home. In this sunken, broken

mouth of a boat, with cracked plates, bent

silverware, all this water rushing in, uninvited.

I have reset the table, cleaned

water swollen floors, removed all hints of dirt. I

have invited guests: whole shining

schools of fish swarm in and out of my new home, one

black octopus has planted her

blooming body at the table's end. I am still

waiting for my reply, from the

sharp silver shark. He swishes his fins, swims sideways,

watches me as I sit to eat.

IV. even if it existed, even if it enlightened

(going up)

i just want to be
closer to that gold
veneer that is my
sky, sparkling even
down here. every
day, i watch the light
filter through all those
miles of cold blue, warm-
ing bodies of fish,
castles of coral
and me. the sea is
so diverse, full of
spiny fish, sharp toothed
eels, waving green sea
weeds, oysters sealed shut.
right now, i must go
slow; careful not to
feel hundreds of pounds
of pressure pressing
my tiny frame. i
wonder what breathing
air again will feel
like, cold or burning?

(existed)

i cannot recall
all the names of all

the people, men and
women, who told me

they would never leave.
i cannot tell you

how many times i've
introduced myself,

how many times i've
seen my mother cry

how many times i've
said, never for me.

(enlightened)

i would like to live
that moment again,

the moment i stopped
hearing my mother's

tone in my voice. it
lasted only one

second. then, i start-
ed wondering, fear-

fully: what if in-
stead of turning in

to her, i started
turning into him?

V. In Opposition to Heaven

Coming to the top was not a straight bullet shot. It was tumbling end over end, spinning like an atom. After a while, I could not tell which part of my body pointed towards the sun.

I did my best.

I eventually came to the top. It gleamed like liquid gold, even though the sun was setting. As I somersaulted towards the surface, I marveled at how impossibly thick it seemed.

I braced for impact.

I expected shards of water to cut through my skin. I expected cold air to flood in my lungs, drowning me. I thought the sun, burning in the distance, would scorch me alive.

None of this happened.

I floated on my back; caught my breath. Half of my body was still submerged in water, trying to resist the undertow. I waited for someone to recognize me, to take me home.

I waited a long time.

Jill Lombardi

You Burn Me

The night is fading my heart
just waking with the sound of your breath
alive and stealing from mine

Let's dance atop the sawdust again
crystal straw still in our hair
curling our hands over each other's hands
the rhythm of crickets

to guide us   a brightening star
a tin lantern I helped make in childhood.

Oh what lovely care
as you reach to fan the flame
your lips beneath my eye
flicker inhale   my lungs inferno

Even the thorns have burst to flames
cherishing every last drop of what I knew.

You are more than the draw of a match
You are a waltz I want to consume me

as slowly as the night   your flame is constant
settling a hand into my hip

Haley Lasché

an ember whispers our pasts quiet.

We are soft, young wood again
loving each other   again and again

falling over the edge
again

From The Twitstat Project

Renee Zepeda

In you the lake moves

legs entwined in your mind's eye

I name the lake me

      "

      when fantasizing
   "   you became
a windshield   "   "
 "   placed carefully
   "   around   "
 " a hybrid
  flower   "my love   "
  is building " a building
 "

   "   around you"   "

quest

m(us)cle
inside a silver (   )
(i)magine (o)pening
(   ) keenly (   ) (   )
we (   ) together
we (o)m

Thinking of three
see you can say Oh
my i hope you'll let me
quote you on that

kneeling in coy cool cowboy boots
i make more almond downtime
hush you honey quick and swoon
the day i came so easily

easily so came i the day
swoon and quick honey hush
downtime almond more make i
boots cowboy kneeling coy

Deaf People Worship S e x I d o l Naked - Breaking N e w s from the Washington Post

Breaking News: In a stunning departure from traditionally established norms, deaf men and women from a c r o s s the nation today cast restraint to the w i n d, stripped down nude, and are now openly worshiping an as-yet unidentified sex idol. Satellite surveillance showed an alleged defiance of cochlear inevitability. The orgy that began at noon yesterday moments ago spilled into the streets after scuffles with beleaguered city law officials, who arrived at the site following an anonymous phone tip alerting authorities to

administrative corruption. T h e scene was so liberating the entire deaf community apparently began letting hands roam beyond established and clearly marked limits! Meanwhile what was thought to be a burning e f f i g y actually turned out to be a dried fecal lump unknown parties "torched for the methane," witnesses said, "to keep the place lit." Reports also tell us that sexual movement did not arise until everyone was packed so closely together, one person's shriek became another's vibration. Drums were beaten and smoked b u r g e r s were served. People began

Christopher Heuer

dancing on "war machines," rolled in for the express purpose of delivering "the final violent thrust." It was only a matter of time before shirts came off, and in the rain, e v e ryone looked good. More fires burned, h u d d l i n g circles tighter. Anyplace o u t s i d e was cold. We asked participants versus spectators (o f t e n one and the same) f o r t h e i r views but wet, clutching fingers dragged away o u r camera, utilizing i t for purposes only selectively broadcasted later, for civil decency.

Matricide

the screams began

when Ace Hardtop

paved over

the Garden of Eden

Matthew Stranach

Still Life with Hands, Wishes and Plate

Chiyuma Elliott

Fold up your limbs my doctors said, cover them
with ice. I cannot use my hands.
They think I have no need of hands.

But if they were yours I asked:
what choices then?
No words came back.

Pencil, if I could hold you again—
the way you dent my middle finger yellow,
I'd dance on the rooftops,

and what I'd make—falling stars,
clover and heather tethered hard to the dirt,
I'd make a swinging bat, I'd send

kisses into the air, and then
I'd make this street, walk down it,
eat a fat red apple. Grin.

Douglas Despres

Zebra

Su Smallen

it's better of course   if you are already one of them,   but if you   look like
one of   them   that's   good, it's   all in how   you look.   that's what
they   move   toward   in their   mergers   and acquisitions. you gotta
come   in with   your str   ipes, five   or seven   years of experi   ence, and
you   gotta flaunt your st   ripes, gotta   get out   there and mingle: network,
net   work! ev   eryone   is useful. lots   of head   nodding and   empty
ges   tures that   all mean   something   as long   as you fit in,   you look
the   part, see   and be   seen, with   blue   chip stock,   doors to
knock,   money   socked,   rainy day,   IRA,   401K, MBA,   UPC, SUV,
equity,   equal   oppor   tunity,   sec   retary,   day plan
ner,   finan   cial plan   ner,   ass   ets, safe   ty nets,
lunch   do   lets.   all this   wealth   can only be   main
tained   in   wealth,   the health   of the com   pany, that is,   the bulk
protec   ted by   the rest.   sure we   lose some   along the way   but that's
good   for in   ventory,   depreci   ation, tax   write-offs, re   structuring,
reor   ganizing,   down   sizing,   that sort   of thing. besides   if you lose
your   stripes   you're   just   not trying   hard enough,   not a part
of   things,   not a   team   player, you   gotta be a   team player
and   every   one's a   referee.   everyone's   replaceable,   see. no
con   science   but the   corpor   ate con   science.   there's al
ways   fresh bl   ood to be   had. ev   erything   here is black   and white.

44

A Girl Named ____

I would write a poem so beautiful that it's simple. Like a plain girl with good brains and nice ways
—Linton Kwesi Johnson, If I Was A Top Notch Poet

You want to meet a girl like this.

A girl more comfortable with a daisy

chain than a circumference of gems

around her neck. A girl who will laugh

hard and doesn't care if you can see her

tonsils. This girl would have been grateful

when flats came back into style if she cared

anything for fashion beyond t-shirts and denim.

This girl remembers your birthday.

Remembers that you like a too-large

dollop of cream with your fresh fruit.

She will lay on her back in the summer

on grass with you, stare at the sky,

make animals of clouds, pocket their names.

She tips generously.

Carries handkerchiefs in her purse.

Always smells a little like lavender.

Her favorite color is blue. Just blue.

She's sweet.

Simple.

Good brains.

Nice ways.

This is the kind of girl you would like

to take home and teach her how to open

Bianca Spriggs

a switchblade fast, when to piss on the potted
plants, what red is the wrong hue to wear
during daylight and how to pull it off.
This is the kind of girl you would like
to teach a tantrum to. How to turn a table over.
How to take another girl home and make her cry.
How to walk in stilettos. Not just walk. Catwalk.
How to inhale. How to down it all in one shot
without making a face. How to make time stop
and things infinitely more complicated for a lover
of plain girls.

Inside Out

If only my insides were outsides
and then you could see the lack of wires
carrying sound into my ears. You
would know not to bother
speaking to my back, whispering in
my ear, calling my cell phone, yelling
when I am in the other room writing
rather than talking even though I can
speak. My voice works perfectly, its
had years of practice, my ears, too, tried
their best. I guess there was a surprise quiz
or two or ten or a hundred
that they failed graciously, lifted
their minute hands, gave in
to the silence, called it poetic,
called it noble, called it art.

Did I spin within the cochlea before
slipping down the Eustachian tube, fall
out my own nose? If my insides were
out, I might be able to get back in, use tweezers
and other instruments, a pen or two,
discover the root of such extraction of a sense
my body apparently didn't think I needed,
didn't see the point, moved on before
I had the chance to adjust properly.

I find myself often outside the things I wish I was inside,
outside groups of loved ones, touching their bodies to replace

the sounds I cannot comprehend, the ways they relate to each
other can only be explained to me later, so I wait
outside their words—
but it's the words I reclaim, the words I want to swallow
like the round windows of my ears, we can still see,
they say, but I am deaf and busy

writing to imagine, writing
to fill in the spaces because I don't want
to be made of space, I am not empty, if my insides
were outsides, then you would see the words
crowding my organs, sailing down blood vessels,
filling me, spilling out.

What of a Body

that cannot lie,
of sinews that do not obey
when commanded to cease
their quaking? What
of a body that scoffs
at holy water's
conditions, of pores
that hunger for
a tongue's fetter,
of nerves deaf
to homilies of *sweet*
by & by & batty bwoy,
boom bye bye? Who
can hold this body
in his hands, silence
its tender, muted moan
beneath scars
that will not heal?

L. Lamar Wilson

Wild You

Matthew Stranach

felt like
running a

pony you

came with spices
from pumpkin

patch you

had fingers to
mend some fences
left to burn away
permafrost

kiss you

grace the corn
fed table of
too many heads
and not enough supper

left from the night
before last went we
through cinnamon chimneys
and matchbook mistakes

crazy you

slip like a ship
through the lips of
those who would

storm you

of what you
got you

taught with
taut and ivory
hands

Writing in English

this is the oppressor's language/ yet I need it to talk to you
—Adrienne Rich, The Burning of Paper Instead of Children

Why struggle to write in the oppressor's language?

Grammar which has chained me
With its lists of rules and wordlinks
Tricky vocabulary with unseen/hidden meanings
And ugly words I learned
They call me and my people
A language which has assertions
That me, my people, are always at 4th grade level

Why do I write in the oppressor's language?

With these black words,
I can reach across timespace
Armless and faceless
To tell you (all of you/us)—

The language is blameless
Like the oppressed,
It needs liberating.
Each poem
is a small victory.

Karen Christie

Scavenger

He looks at me
with penetrating eyes
Seeking the deepest part of my soul
Where the I
Unbeknownst to me
lies.
His quest?
To claim me as his own.

With a stealthy agenda,
this creature,
encroaching
walking in bold confidence—
arrogance in disguise
plots my demise.

His hand touches mine,
He leads me to his side
His choice
Out of the pageantry
Ah, he noticed me...
How could this be?
Finally!

Zendrea Mitchell

All too complaisant
Transfixed
Mesmerized
All caution pushed aside
With each step closer
My internal temperature rises,
Prospering increased naivety,
Unwittingly, I welcome him inside.

There, his grasp
Initially,
...ohhhh...so soft, so tender
suddenly
tenacious
pulling
he finds my Joy
and replaces it with sorrow
He takes my Strength
I am left with pain
My loving heart
Belittled
Now numb
He takes my Faith
And gives me doubt
Who am I?
Am I no longer myself?

Contemplating my demise
Becoming smaller with time
As he tramps on my heart, body and mind
What have I done?
I was just looking to be loved.

He continues to dig
To cleave
Until he beholds
Nestled
Rooted
Planted
My seed...
The essence of me.

Surrounded by a crimson darkness,
Pushing through a once tenable sheath,
His hand,
as he tries one last time
a light blinds him
Reflecting into mine
I see a glimpse of what I used to be
And long to retrieve what was taken from me.

Language Lesson

Ashaki M. Jackson

The mouth opens like a grave

*

Our mouths open like her grave

*

Our mouths: her grave   thick-
tongued cavern   From our throats she blooms
Sunday hymn toward a quiet sky

*

Thick-tongued quiet   Our mouths
caverns   graves   Our throats
bloom a Sunday sky hymn

*

Throat hymns
The sky: a grave of tongues
Thick blooms quiet our cavernous mouths
like a Sunday

*

Our mouths   Our
mouths   Our mouths
Our mouths   quiet

And sky

Darkness

I very alone in home I sit on couch and I saw picture frame on wall start I cry person
is gone I say goodbye to person I have hard in my life person is left without me lonely
every day have time I walk in forest beautiful sky night with many star anywhere I stand
around in forest enough darkness wait I can feel person with me you need to go back
home fast falling sleep your eyes close blackness next day morning open your eyes
light shine I saw person come with me hold hand we walk to forest get big smile I have
Strength, Power, and Courage once I have darkness I never lost balance it true person
give me save my life when I feel tired we hope get brave I can make it through no more
scared myself I still tear can't stop pain my heart must present brave and memories
remember wonderful person have lovely you will have big sweet dream everyone now
know it happiness find my way allowing me forever in way dream blessing peace them
open heart dream is safe perfect anyone of life already born or not yet born need accept
life have gift everyone I see beautiful sunrise and sunset what you want future and goal
yesterday and tomorrow every day I promise person hope better promise on tomorrow
I saw many butterfly in my heart forever I feel one drop water soon come rain dance
myself saw rainbow darkness bring dream rain change sunshine to everyone, you and
me I walk forest and I saw my name on nature I never forget forest, waterfall, butterfly,
and earth I saw pink rose don't pick rose if you pick rose become black mess up sleep not
wake up until 3 days wake up you have choice don't pick rose or pick rose please don't
tear should pain my heart how feel I saw waterfall with rock smell very good fresh I walk
on road wait until dark night walk go home not open your eyes fast falling sleep lie on
bed your eyes close never forget and still remember take your time sleep head on pillows
hope have, think can do and perfect big sweet dream remember in true dream sleep your
hand hold on heart is cold need hold heart become it
this heart is warm.

Tara Lee Bautista

Chance

She flirted with sin
And only the moon saw
Too bad the moon has eyes for all

Autumn Joy Jimerson

Douglas Despres

Family Conversations

Raymond Luczak

Had they the right ears to hear
the rumbling inside my stomach's pit?
No matter what they fed me,
I still went hungry after dessert.
My hearing aids weren't enough.
They didn't want to ask too deeply
what had starved me: the questions.
They continued to babble the table,
and I simply sat there, trying to eat
mouthfuls of misunderstanding.
Nothing said was ever important.
If my ears turned silent and inward,
they said to open the lid of sounds.
Then nothing said was ever important.
The table was oval, expandable.
The rules were. My ears were not.
I stared at their faces, their mouths
gabbering amidst handfuls of words.
The tongues pushing aside chunks
just to stuff a slice of word in edgewise
were pink with raw jealousy.
My stomach, empty with coldness,
kept shivering while it bloated
a hunger insatiable at their table.

It Sits on Them, Like Eggs

The small lake where I used to
skip rocks
is a two-story house now.

It should look the same
as every other two-story house
on the block

but it doesn't.

Keith Wilson

Exorcisms I Have Tried

Kimberly Eridon

reading about pain	not reading about pain
not talking about pain	talking about pain
	talking too much about pain
metaphors	similes
reading stories	writing stories
physical therapy	inactivity
rest	exercise
cruelty to others	and myself
adaptability	stubbornness
science	art
novels	graphic novels
fairy tales	prayers
blaming others	martyrdom
anger	reading
halfhearted research papers	impassioned essays
rage	acceptance
giving up	hope

searching for meaning	abandoning the search for meaning
music	silence
random movement	cautious stillness
frustration	grief
crankiness	carefully maintained neutrality
poetry	vicious caricatures
naïveté	cynicism
pity for the oppressors	sympathy for the oppressed
vanity	self effacement
imagining making a difference	doing nothing
friends	thinking too much
	stopping myself from thinking too much

self-control	tears
asking the oppressors why	not asking God why
	asking God what
	am I supposed to do
	with this

hope

Note from a Prodigal Son I

Randall Horton

Father,   there are yellow

      clusters,   paper balls

piled   wastebasket high,

      useless attempts   at reconciliation.

Somehow   you & I   need

      to close   this empty

space   between   us.

      I devoured   a dictionary,

yet words   still—

      mysterious drawings.

A legal pad   stares

      stoically,   refusing

to interpret   knots

clogging my throat.   The brutality

of isolation,   it's not easy,

    this upheaval—

Vice(s)

Daniel O. Harris

Vice(s)

Vice(s)

He used to tell me
"put it **in the vice**"
and shook my hand
so hard **it hurt**

but I was **tough**
I **squeezed** back
Ignoring the **pain**

He used to **tell** me
"grab me a beer"
and I would **toss** him
the **Grain Belt** from the fridge

but I was **tough**
I **squeezed** back
Ignoring the pain

66

White Shoes

I know men.
Men who are poets.
Black poets who wear
White shoes.

Basketball shoes
Worn only to workshops;
Spotless white shoes
Worn at open mics.

When these men stand,
Rooms grow quiet.
When these men speak,
Rooms listen.

Flannery O'Connor
Says no man
With a good car needs
To be justified.

What she must think
Of all these black poets—
Beautiful black poets
In their shoes.

Destiny Birdsong

What is a Sign Language Poem?

Donna Williams

What is a Sign Language poem?
It's a living, moving thing;
my hands swirl in air,
the Signs flow and sing.

My face gives all away;
am I happy, excited, sad?
My body emphasises;
was this thing good or bad?

A poem on the page
with words prettily aligned
has its own skill and beauty,
but it's not the same as Sign.

Words are static, unmoving;
dead, laid out for all to see.
Signs are living, breathing;
my poems live in me.

I know what I want to say;
in Sign, it's so clear.
But trying to translate my poems
fills me with fear.

I want to create on paper
what I feel on the stage,
but writing down my poems
seems like putting them in a cage.

The words are never right,
they never say what I mean,
yet I see them in my head;
it's almost like a dream.

Imagine you have a painting;
A Monet, a Van Gogh, a Vermeer.
Try and copy it with crayons;
picture frustration and tears.

My poems flow and breathe,
they fill the space they're in.
To capture them with a pen
is to nail them down with ink.

They struggle and resist
until they lie, defeated, on the page.
And all I can think when I look at it
is that it looks better on the stage.

Words are static, unmoving;
dead, laid out for all to see.
Signs are living, breathing;
my poems live in me.

Self Consciousness

Kimberly Eridon

(3)

When I was a child, I would lie in the bathtub trying to keep the water from draining out, so I could keep singing in the warm and resonant space created by five sides of bathtub/shower and one side partly of shower curtain. I would sing whatever came to mind, usually songs of praise to God, sort of improvisational worship with a wandering tune meandering with my warm thoughts. I was relaxed and sleepy, and my mother came in and scared me half to consciousness and said how good my made-up song was, and I was embarrassed, and I could not do that anymore without knowing someone could be listening, so I got up dried off got dressed went to bed and never sang like that again.

(4)

I loved the different
sounds a human voice could make,

and when I was younger, I would talk in different voices while I
did chores, usually on Saturday mornings when I was alone.

I would stage little conversations that would go wherever my thoughts did,
sometimes in unexpected directions, and I would wonder where they came from.

One day, my mother must have been
in the other room, and I didn't know it,

but she must have heard me because she came
half-running into the kitchen while I was dusting

the family room, and she said she heard voices, and
did I hear anything, and I lied and said,

"I didn't hear a thing," and she said,
"I was afraid it might be demons,"

and I wonder now if she was joking,
but at the time I thought she was serious,

so unless I was the only one in the house,
I didn't talk anymore when I did my chores

because I was afraid of being demons.

Me My Hearing Aids

Zendrea Mitchell

Stepping inside the tightly lit room with dark corners,

my heart beating faster than my steps

I held my father's hand.

We sat.

Towering over us the AUDIOLOGIST

smiled

mouthing incoherently.

In her hands, she held a petite green box.

Within held a treasure that would encase sounds.

Removing the treasure, she lifted it up to the light—

bringing it onto the surface of my brown skin

Its tad nuance of color would camouflage it from wayward eyes.

Her fingers sent a chill through my bones

as she inspected inside the darkness for unsuspecting visitors.

All was clear.

She slipped the clear, close to invisible mold

that would eventually turn yellow into my ears.

It eased into the hollow pit.

A perfect fit.

With a swift movement of her thumb,

she clicked it on...

eeeeeeeeeeeeeeeeeeeeeeeee...it hissed.

Quickly, she lowered the volume a notch.

Smiling, she looked at my father looking at me,

earnestly.

He let go of my hands.

He said four words, now a perpetual repugnance,

"Do you hear me?"

Hiding behind the crescent moon,
lost in a world of sound
as my heart played
its first of many roles,
I said,
"Yes."

Revenant

Khary Jackson

The body does not know what world
it lives in. This is why when I dream of falling
from a cliff, my body shocks awake,
heart blasting a scream it no longer needs.
Where the soul moves, the body will follow.

When your dream returned, on my way out
of my office, at work, just before my hand reached
the door, my tired body remembered you:
Lying on our sides, in someone's bed,
you had lain your cheek in my left hand.

When your dream returned to me
in my office, at work, my heart rioted
in reflex, my veins swelling
from the breath that rose in.
I was angry for only then waking up.

My body rooted itself through the carpet,
felt me leaving, preparing itself to fall.

My left hand is the soil you left so quietly
open. My left hand still believes it is there,
in some room where you are alive,
this left-brain blasphemy.

My left hand does not age. It has not surrendered
a cell of dead skin. It does not waste its grip
calling the soul back.

Solace Against Emptiness

solace against emptiness

vision will   influence frail

transparent. . . sprawling   rubble

absurd and anxious

chaos

continues its settled   listening

wild rainfall   solace

against menacing

agony

mosaic–morsel

Sandy Beach

dreams a semblance

                                        of evils
        lesser than
emptiness

                hail   storm commands
                pressured   woe in

                                    the perturbed air
                pungent ivy–toxin
                            hollow   time
                                        billows
            swaddled odes

Dactylology

Here, right before your eyes, is a textbook:
resin, thread, cardboard, and sheets of paper
cut to size so it all feels smooth. Even
the text leaves behind tattoos of sensation
when you rake lightly against the words.
Everything's the same no matter what the page is.

Over here's a pair of hands: bone, blood, skin.
Words are fingerspelled, a lightning of handshapes
representing the letters of the alphabet. Sometimes
you'll wonder just what is it that you've seen.
Nothing's ever the same twice. Hands are alive,
breathing, veins throbbing with language.

Textbooks exude authority, experiments, statistics.
One must become dispassionate and skeptical.
Hands are flighty, unreliable, tactile, and feral.
They got one thing that research doesn't have:
blood pumping both love and hate, and the in-between
stuff that keep us awake with dreams gone speechless.

Raymond Luczak

The Last Morning

Sarah Roesler Conbere

Fog stretches her thin fingers

along open, deep blue water

pleated and sporadically flared

amongst striding tipped waves

Our animal presence glides, no

breaches, rolls her spine—

water break and I glimpse her

beneath this arctic velvet

in concentration. A dark rainbow

has crowned your head—

three times. A call

that ripples like a party dress

We push pull our kayak

aim our nose toward sloping shore

subsides to brother/sister who

is the sky. I turn as I hear

shimmery night skin fold gracefully

as you stare ahead

not 10 feet behind

a momentary glow of being

Jill Lombardi

Things I Know Like the Back of My Hand

My mom is sometimes embarrassed about her hands,
they look more like a man's hands she says
holding them in front of her at arm's length.
She means the short nails, the swollen knuckles.
She means the years of work that made them so.

I'm sometimes embarrassed about my hands.
They give out without warning, they drop things—
cups, forks, books. And they're slow to listen.
Yesterday, I only wanted half a glass of juice
but they took their sweet time. My glass is always full.

My mom worries a lot about my hands
but she's also relieved. I'll never sit all day
at a sewing machine making sheepskin slipcovers,
or stretch and staple webbing that cuts my skin.
It's a blessing she says when something clatters to the floor.

Chiyuma Elliott

Zulaikha: On Falling

There's a dream that I believe/When I wake up it goes away
—Sunday Valley, I Don't Mind

begins with the gray hour.
downpour.
e dawn sun.
    Walking trees.
    A caul of fog.
slow procession—

shadow sewn into a hem.

ere are no fingerprints here.
    There are no numbers.
    Only ceremony—a blizzard—
    blossoms falling over an orchard
    of upturned, veiled faces.
    Someone is a bride today.
meone's mouth will be empty of rice.
    Someone will be born an ancestor.
ear this bell, a drum, a slow sweet wind,
oice paddling through a lake

that was once a grove of spirits,
cut loose,
wondering how
anything could ever end.

First, there's a lasso
And you're drowning.
No, first you're drowning,
then there's a lasso,
but I do not save you.
You are too heavy.
Instead.
I save a locket full of your hair
that's been bitten in half.
Now I have a tooth wandering
as loose as a wraith in a hainthouse.
Then there's blood spilt
    from your palm.
I mark my forehead with it
    in a complex line.
Paint it gold.
I make a vow.
Break it.
There is a white tent in a desert of red.
    Too much red.

You let go first.

For some reason
I don't mind.

I am young.
Too young to remember much
except falling for something
    bright in the water.
    Then there are hands.
Dark brown and big as wings.
My mother's mouth floats
    above the wings, a vowel

    blurred by light.

Seconds rob me of my life.
    I do not care.

I am something new.
The sky is a mirage.

My hair tangles in fronds
    growing beside me.

You crawl inside my shell.

A dream sets us

    adrift.

Bianca Spriggs

Given

at eleven
she gives me her shell
tells me she's done with it
i put it up to my ear, hear
the sound of her leaving

Kelli Stevens Kane

Ed Bock

Stones Formerly Known as Love

Michelle Whittaker

It is passing
                    like a stone through a window,
          a knob through a door glassy,
                              an iris through light,
          shifts through a stare,
                    a bedspring through beating,
                                   a spread is passing bread on table,
as cocked is stirring untouched,
                         a gold ring is passing through my legs
                                        as a teacher passes out a test.
                         a love story passes through you. several times in fact,
as I watch the passing driver run on through a Stop.

Jill Lombardi

Spiral Grounding

ONE: OVEREXPOSED

"[ ] an image of a landscape captured, but too much."

Mark Luyten

Sandy Beach

truth evades a self composed of half–truths
views pray to be seen not scenic

dream unfolding obsession   besotted prior engagements
composed otherworldly ventures
smudge only signifying

precariously posed places
overexposed super8mm
images stained to whiteness

snow–blind soundtrack   scritching beyond rhythm
Vonnegut-witted   posed as if canvas–primed
impressively scant   carte blanche   not   carte vista

'Lost' is not 'never existed'

TWO: PROCESSION

circling aslant climb
solid pretense of normalcy
            savor primal urging
laden invocation
dismissing all plausible
futures or pasts

latent explanations
gravel grit steps founder
at the edge of sulfurous O
emergent in 79 A.D.
grounding all for posterity

shoes path blue pant legs stone
staggering in–out of frame
this singular obsession
details a narrative spiral
earth whose time is light
light time earth

*Inspired by Mark Luyten's accidentally overexposed, "white film"
and "Walking Around the Vesuvius Crater" (1994) and On a
Balcony: A Novel, which I accidentally discovered at Goodwill.*

Christopher Heuer

Bitter/Better

bitter   bitter
 bitte   r   b   itter
   bit ter   bit ter
   bit ter   bit ter
     bit   ter   bit
     ter   bitter   bitt
   er bi   tter bitter   bitt
 er bit   ter bitter bit   ter b
 itter   bitter bitter   bitter
 bitt   er bitter b   itter
   bitter   bitter   bitter
   bitter   bitter   bitter
     bitter   bitter bitter   bitter
     bitter   bitter bitter bitter   bitter
      bitter bi   tter bitter bitter bitte   r bitter
   bitter bitter   bitter bitter   bitter bitter bitter bi
     ter bitter bi   tter bitter bitter   bitter bitter bitter
     bitter bitter bitter bitter bit   ter bitter bitter
     bitter bitteer bitter bitter b   e   tter bitter bitt
       er bitter bitter bitter bitte   r bitter bitter b
       ter bit ter bitter bitter b   itter bitter bit
         ter bitter bitter bitter bit ter bitter bitte
           r bitter bitter bitter bitter bitter bitter b
       itte   r bitter bitter bitter bitter bitter
                     bitter bitter bitter bitter bit
                   ter bitter bitter bitter bit
                     bitter bitter bitter bit
                   ter bitter bitter bit
                   ter bitter bitter bi
                   ter bitter bitter b
                   itter bitter bitter bit
                 ter bitter bitter bitter b
                 itter bitter bitter bitter b
                 itter bitter bi tter bitter bi
                 tter bitter bi   ter bitter bi
                 tter bitter b   itter bitter b
                 itter bitte   r bitter bitter
                 bitter bit   ter bitter b
                   itter bit   ter bitter b
                   itter bit   ter bitter
                   bitter b itter bit
                 ter bit ter bit
   ter   bitter bitter bit ter bitter   bit
 ter bitter bitter bitter bitter bitter bitter bitter b
   itter bitter bitter bitter bitter bitter bitter
     bitter bitter bitter   bitter bitter bitter

89

Douglas Despres

One Deed Another Begets

black barrel

                            i aim

      the bull's-eye   falling a robin

motionless

                          feathers flutter

      slowly   it happens

decades later

                   on a stoop

      this time   i sit

still

                     a humming

      girl's   voice   cries out

as if   i know

                 why-oh-why

      o piercing   a bullet

has to

                   memory

      time & death   beget

coincidences

      inseparable of   the deed.

Randall Horton

Instead, a Tiny Metal Elephant

Rachel Fogarty-Oleson

I.

She will come back—in her wake, your empty room, white space.
          This is the ebb, the narrative upside down, roots gasping
for air, the new routine. And like a tree stretched
          across a milkshake sky, you embody the flexibility
of a contortionist. Whole, fluid, even your footsteps are pillows;
          though, this time, this move, this man was different,
and she forgot to remember you.   A moth danced across the
          yellow porch light as she turned to go.

II.

Here, step-mothers are worse than evil. The eggs already broken
          in their carton, and ears clench like a fisted heart. Vertigo.
Unclipped tongues tie to wooden crosses, and his eyes,
          his lake-wide eyes flicker with distrust—smudged
by another's hand. He is a foreign, an irregular heartbeat. He
likes the color orange and wants to eat bananas for breakfast.

III.

Promises, difficult in their obviousness, slide down unblinking
          cheeks. She smiles right at his face. The hem of the sky
neatly folds into its corner, the edges complete. Getting in the way
          of goodbyes, one caught in between two, he presses into
my palm, a tiny metal elephant. The last warm thing of his that I
will touch.

The Floater

I have yet to learn how to hurricane the trees like him,
        bend their necks down until the snap
then migration hidden in all the wrong, wrong spaces.
I watched the boats unstrapped, one by none left on the back waters
      like an unbeliever from a billy-goat stare
between his hand and the wild fever away. I saw him do it.
  Some nights I try to hide the writhe,
     even when striding fingers over ears, I can still hear him,
      as a river does trying to keep a royal tone over rocks
   but I can't stop un-strapping the back waters in replay
       while minding the owl who pushes through these rural parts
 I'm learning to mind that cockerel head, I'm learning who twisted this man thin
as a kite strung high up the wrong, wrong bark.

Michelle Whittaker

Post-Modern

I overdosed today on words,
was life supported
by hate alone.

Why should this be, back floating
Like back yard swimming pools
or Viking funeral pyres?

If love is not enough,
what's God to do when he's done
twiddling his thumbs?

Omnipresence is so strange,
Getting mentioned even
in the Godless way

of hearing passion sizzle—
evaporate soul
like pork fat on a grill.

Keith Wilson

Ed Bock

Insertion

Curtis Robbins

I

Hearing
Implosive sound rushing
from a hearing aid.
The corrupted, the eroded—
those deadened hairs in the cochlea—
the nautilus of the mind
acrimoniously tormented
by the push of megaphonic vibrations
spiraling through—
unheard of.

Acoustic highs
raging plucks from noises
leave whispering tones—
unheard of.

It's beyond incomprehensible.

Take it off!
What's the use
of dizzy tintinnabulations—
unheard of.

II

Silence in the dark
I lie on a gurney
until Meniere's ding
a groggy reawakening.

My head bandaged.
My mouth dry—
begging for the mercy of an ice-cold drink
growling for a few saltines
struggling to stay awake—
struggling to fall back asleep.

Scampering nurses
a momentary surgeon
making curtain calls—
checking for assurances

I hardly had the strength to applaud.

III

A magnetic button aside the auricle
none of that irritation inserted
through the ear canal.
Sounds came through
hardly a holler
but a roar
unheard of.

Squeaks and beeps
voices of Donald Duck
out so many mouths—
unheard of.

Sound—
a different
a strange
a new different
a new strange—
a new set of acclimations to amend.
Not like the hearing aid catching the rapping—
but waiting for knockdown resounding
of uninviting banters.

IV

Sounds of music dancing
Speedy swishes
Honks and beeps
Chirps and tweets
Buzzes and chortles
Bangs and sweeps
Twerps and burps
unheard of.

Dad! Tea kettle! Dad?

Sips and slurps
Squished teabag
A spoonful tingle
A cupful jingle.

The Dizzy Gillespie Test

Daniel O. Harris

<u>Dizzy</u>   <u>Test</u>

I check to make sure

        pray to look like
trumpet player

        half a man

ironic
   share its name

       bells in my ears
       palsy days.

        do a mean
Elvis
snarl

growl

half-hearted

<u>The Dizzy Gillespie Test</u>

For a number of years now
I check to make sure it is still
gone. I hold my finger up to my
lips and blow. I pray to look like
that trumpet player with both
cheeks filling with air. I don't
ever want to feel like half a man
again.

It is ironic that this affliction
should share its name with a
ringing musical instrument. If I
close both my eyes (now) I can
still hear the bells in my ears
during those palsy days.

I remember I could do a mean
Elvis when I had it. I had the
snarl down pat. "Thank you,
thank you very much," I would
growl as I shook my hips like the
king. It would get an expected
half-hearted laugh from my
concerned family and friends.

an eye patch.
see my left eye
                blink.

                face joked,

the left laid limp
        tears
        inside.

        puff my cheeks

                easy to forget
    numb

    lose part

                whole
again.

I had to wear an eye patch. You see my left eye needed protection from its inability to blink. I was a regular swashbuckling pirate. The right side of my face joked, mimicked, and laughed. While the left laid limp with an inability to shed the tears that were welling up inside.

So, today I puff my cheeks and close my eyes and make sure I am complete. It is easy to forget, get numb to, ailments that don't affect you personally. But, once you lose part of yourself even for a short time you always want to make sure that you are whole again.

It's Just That the Sun
Has Bones Made of People

Hafizah Geter

i must admit you shout like a trench coat.
what i am trying to say is that,

i have been mauling bears. been throwing pillows through glass.
you might say spoons are the only company i keep.

it's not that i lie, but the truth has been standing around,
pouring wine in its mouth. drunker than a gazebo,

it's habitual. that there's something between the avenue,
thunder in the crockpot.

what gathers now is a decoy.

Recurring Eargasm

rapid taps on the windowpane rattle

                  brilliantly   i think it b. the turntablist   mixing

                      sleet & rain falls   hysterical till noon

i check my wristwatch   on the way out   to the tick-tock

i don't stop the screen door from slamming   my umbrella dangles

                       side to side the m.c. wave your hands   says—damn

lower the volume   in the house down to one   i forgot

by one the bus leaves   surely this audio will

                       fade to that resonant frequency   in yr earhole

soon i will b.   back at the crib   inside the rattle

Randall Horton

Last

this   this   this   could be my last syllable
a city lives within me but
I don't really know which city
just that there are tubes in it.
speaking of tubes
I found my ear canal in a tuba
and I found my throat in a chimney.
the body is a trap we each get caught in
this   this   this   could be my last body.

Kelli Stevens Kane

Meghan Maloney-Vinz

CONTRIBUTORS

Tara Lee Bautista grew up deaf in a hearing family in Hollister, CA. Some family members know Sign Language. Tara currently lives in Willows, CA. She was very close to her grandmother, Rosalie Bautista, who died when Tara was four years old. Tara attended California School for the Deaf - Fremont, CA, from age seven to twenty and graduated in the class of 2006. Her poem, Darkness, was written in December of 2009.

Sandy Beach's poetry has landed her in Italy with Ezra Pound's family, L.A., Dallas, D.C., and Chicago. Broadsides of her work are available at redbirdchapbooks.com. Poems appear in mnartists.org, What Light Poetry Project!, mentalcontagion.org, Perigee Publication for the Arts, To Sing Along the Way: Minnesota Women Poets, and Water~Stone Review. The poem Idiosyncratic Runes first appeared in a chapbook, Dreamcasting: A Response to Forest Walk. She lives in Minneapolis.

Destiny Birdsong is a Cave Canem fellow and a graduate of Vanderbilt University and received her MFA in Creative Writing (Poetry) and a PhD in Literature. She is currently working on a manuscript that is tentatively titled, Scald.

Ed Bock lives in Minneapolis, MN with Mary, his sweet wife, Hannah, the cat who runs the household, twelve fish tanks in the basement, three small fish ponds in the backyard and an ever-growing garden that may one day make lawn mowing obsolete. In the ordinary world around him are dramatic discoveries to explore, creations (stuff) to make, and life to be appreciated, enjoyed and shared.

Karen Christie (name-sign "KC") grew up in California and has been a professor of Deaf Cultural Studies and English at the National Technical Institute for the Deaf at Rochester Institute of Technology. Along with Patti Durr, she produced and edited a multimedia DVD set, The HeART of Deaf Culture: Literary and Artistic Expressions of Deafhood. Most of her writings have appeared/disappeared in her trash, although some have made it into Deaf Lit Extravaganza, The Tactile Mind Quarterly and Clerc Scar.

Douglas Despres is passionate about documentary photography and is based out of Alameda, CA. He loves meeting new people and recording them within their element. A decade of experience has afforded him exposure in everything from museums to music magazines, and has taken him across the U.S. and abroad to Cuba, Thailand, Costa Rica, and Italy.

Chiyuma Elliott lives in Oakland, CA, with her husband and two noisy dogs. She is a Stegner Fellow in Poetry at Stanford University, and a Visiting Scholar in English at the University of California, Berkeley. In fall of 2013, she became Assistant Professor of English and African American Studies at the University of Mississippi.

Kimberly Eridon writes about whatever catches her attention in whatever form(s) the content seems to call for. She loves lines and the spaces between and outside of them as well as margins, white space, and the printed word in general. She is also addicted to reading.

Rachel Fogarty-Oleson received support from the Hampton Arts Management Micro-Grant and was the 2010 recipient of the Thomas E. Sanders Scholarship in Creative Writing Award. She serves on the editorial board of Yellow-Jacket Press. Her poems and new media poetic pieces have appeared in numerous journals and presses, such as Extract(s), 30/30 Tupelo Press Project, OVS Magazine, Psychic Meatloaf, White Space Poetry Anthology, and espresso ink. She is also the curator for City Gallery at Brooksville City Hall.

Jessica Fox-Wilson is a part-time poet and a full-time educator. She earned a Bachelor of Arts in Creative Writing and Middle-Secondary Education at Beloit College in Beloit, WI, and a Master of Fine Arts in Writing at Hamline University, in St. Paul, MN. She published her first poetry collection, Blameless Mouth, through Everything Feeds Process Press, available on Lulu and Amazon. Some of her poems have appeared in several journals, including Gin Bender, Blind Man's Rainbow and qarrtsiluni, and her articles about poetry and literature have appeared in Read Write Poem and the Uptown Neighborhood News. She lives in Minneapolis with her husband and daughter.

Hafizah Geter is a South Carolina native currently living in Brooklyn, NY. She holds an MFA from Columbia College Chicago and is a Cave Canem Fellow. Her poems have appeared or are forthcoming in Columbia Poetry Review, RHINO, New Delta Review, Boxcar Poetry Review, NANO Fiction, and Drunken Boat.

Daniel O. Harris is a graduate of the Master's program at Hamline University in St. Paul, MN. His creativity happens in many forms – poetry, creative non-fiction, screenplays, haiku, Volkswagen restoration, etc. He likes to think of himself as a well-rounded writer who is proud of his unfocused dabbling style. He lives in Brooklyn Park, MN with his wife, Julie, and daughters, Anna & Elizabeth.

Christopher Heuer is the author of Bug: Deaf Identity and Internal Revolution and All Your Parts Intact: Poems. His creative work and political essays have additionally appeared in The Tactile Mind Quarterly, Kaleidoscope Magazine, Wordgathering-A Journal of Disability Poetry, Breath and Shadow Magazine, voiceofsandiego.org, The Endeavour, journalgazette.net, and several anthologies (Deaf American Prose: 1980-2010, Deaf American Poetry: An Anthology, The Deaf Way II Anthology, and No Walls of Stone). He is the Editor in Chief of Deafecho.com and an Associate Professor of English at Gallaudet University. He lives in Virginia with his wife Amy and his son Jack.

Randall Horton is the author of The Definition of Place and the Lingua Franca of Ninth Street, both from Main Street Rag. Randall is the recipient of the Gwendolyn Brooks Poetry Award, the Bea Gonzalez Poetry Award and most recently a National Endowment of the Arts Fellowship in Literature. His creative and critical work has most recently appeared in Callaloo, Crab Orchard Review, and The Packingtown Review. Randall is a Cave Canem Fellow, a member of the Affrilachian Poets and a member of The Symphony: The House that Etheridge Built. He has an MFA in Poetry from Chicago State University and a PhD in Creative Writing from SUNY Albany. Randall is Assistant Professor of English at the University of New Haven.

Ashaki M. Jackson is a Cave Canem poetry fellow and a member of the Voices of Our Nations Arts (VONA) writing community. Her work has appeared or is forthcoming in publications including Eleven Eleven, Suisun Valley Review, and Generations Literary Journal. She is currently a social psychologist and program evaluator for initiatives involving teen girls in Greater Los Angeles.

Khary Jackson is a performance poet, playwright, dancer and musician. A Detroit native, he currently resides in the Twin Cities where he serves as a teaching artist and writer. He is a Cave Canem Fellow, and as a result has further reason to adore black people. Khary is the author of a book of poems, Any Psalm You Want (Write Bloody, 2011). He has written 12 full length plays, one of which (Water) was produced in

2009 at Ink and Pulp Theatre in Chicago. He has been a recipient of several grants, including the 2010 Artist Initiative Grant for poetry from The Minnesota State Arts Board, and the Many Voices Residency at the Playwrights' Center, in 2005 and 2007. As a performance poet, he has enjoyed great success in national competition and won the National Poetry Slam with the St. Paul team in 2009 and 2010.

Autumn Joy Jimerson, holds an M.S. in Marriage and Family Therapy from Loma Linda University and a B.A. in Communications from Howard University. Currently residing in Los Angeles, Autumn continues to uphold her appreciation for the creative process, serving as both a writer and therapist.

Haley Lasché has her MFA from Hamline University. Her poems and essays have appeared in many lit mags, anthologies and websites such as Not a Muse, Poemeleon, and Dossier Journal. In addition to writing, she is a college instructor, a post-modern dancer and a punk-rock fashion model.

Jill Lombardi has a Bachelor of Arts from the University of Minnesota. As part of her undergraduate studies, Jill completed a year's study abroad program at the University of Bologna, Italy, where she discovered her passion for photography.

Her photographic style gravitates to vibrant colors and dramatic black and whites. She is based in Southern California as a natural light portrait photographer where she lives with her husband and two children.

Raymond Luczak's five books of poems are St. Michael's Fall (Deaf Life Press, 1996), This Way to the Acorns: The 10th Anniversary Edition (Handtype Press, 2012), Mute (A Midsummer Night's Press, 2010), Road Work Ahead (Sibling Rivalry Press, 2011), and How to Kill Poetry (Sibling Rivalry Press, 2013). His other books include Assembly Required: Notes from a Deaf Gay Life (RID Press, 2009), Silence is a Four-Letter Word: On Art & Deafness [The 10th Anniversary Edition] (Handtype Press, 2012), and Men with Their Hands: A Novel (Queer Mojo, 2009). A playwright and filmmaker, he lives in Minneapolis. (raymondluczak.com)

Meghan Maloney-Vinz taught high school English for eight years before pursuing an MFA in poetry at Hamline University. She is the Managing Editor for the literary journal, Water~Stone Review, and director of the Hamline Young Writers Workshop. Meghan is also the business manager for the collaborative publishing guild, Broadcraft Press. She is a maker/fixer, according to her nine year old. That is just about spot on.

Zendrea Mitchell or Zen, as sometimes called by close family and friends, graced the stage and camera with a Zen-like ambiance as an actor and signed musical performing artist. She is a Mother, Daughter, Sister, Poet, ASL Songstress, and Advocate. She graduated from Syracuse University with a BA degree in English, and studied Theater at the National Theater of the Deaf and Deaf West Theater. Most recently, she was cast in multiple roles in the theater production of The Vagina Monologues and appeared in the short film, Night Sky. As a poet, she wrote poems in her slim black book about life, love, and immersing/straddling the worlds of the deaf/hearing. She is featured in the short film, White Space.

Marisa Quinn believes in a natural, intuitive approach to image capture. The most essential component of her work is having a true connection to her subjects and the space they are inhabiting. She has lived and worked in New York, Austin, Los Angeles, Puebla, Mexico, London and Italy. (marisaqphotography.com)

Kristen Ringman is a deaf writer, sailor, traveler, and new mother. She is the author of Makara (Handtype Press, 2012), a literary lyrical novel about the deaf daughter of an Irish selchie who falls in love with a girl in South India. Her poetry has been published in Deaf Lit Extravaganza, Deaf American Poetry: An Anthology, Wordgathering, and The Poet's Place: A Collection of Works. She received her MFA from Goddard College in 2008 and has attended A Room of Her Own Women's Writing Retreats in 2011 and 2013. Besides poetry, she is currently writing a YA science fiction trilogy set in SE Asia. (kristenringman.com) (balancingbetween.wordpress.com)

Curtis Robbins is a graduate of Gallaudet University, and a retired adjunct professor, who taught – among other things – American Sign Language and Deaf Culture for over 40 years prior to his retirement in 2007. Robbins has published several poems found in four anthologies: No Walls of Stone (1982), The Deaf Way II Anthology (2002), Deaf American Poetry (2009), and Deaf Lit Extravaganza (2013). Several other poems are found online, in several Deaf and non-Deaf publications, and in several textbooks on Deaf Culture. He lives in Maryland with his wife, Susan, and has two grown children.

Sarah Roesler Conbere's poetry has appeared in journals such as Main Channel Voices, The Talking Stick, and Sage Trail, as well as anthologies, What Light and Along the Rio Grande. She has also participated with Talking Image Connection in Minneapolis, Minnesota. An English teacher by profession, she enjoys traveling outside of the school year. She holds her M.F.A. in Writing from Hamline University.

Su Smallen is the author of Buddha, Proof, a Minnesota Book Award Finalist, and Weight of Light, nominated for the Pushcart Press Editor's Book Award. Other honors include the Jane Kenyon Poetry Prize and a Joy Harjo Prize. Su's poems and essays appear in many journals, anthologies, and chapbooks, notably Collecting Life: Poets on Objects Known and Imagined, Midway Journal, The Normal School, The Quiet Eye: Thirteen Ways of Looking at Nature, Water~Stone Review, and the White Space Poetry Anthology. She was a founding member of the Laurel Poetry Collective, making beautiful and affordable books and broadsides for ten years. Formerly a professional choreographer and dancer, Su and her poetry were featured in the documentary dance film Klatch. Currently, she is an editor at the University of Minnesota Law School Institute on Crime and Public Policy and director of the writing center at St. Olaf College. Su lives in St. Paul, Minnesota with her poodle, Rococo. (susmallen.com)

Bianca Spriggs is an Affrilachian Poet, Cave Canem Fellow, and a freelance instructor of composition, literature, and creative writing. She holds degrees from Transylvania University and the University of Wisconsin. She is a recipient of an Artist Enrichment Grant from the Kentucky Foundation for Women, and the creator and programmer of the Gypsy Poetry Slam featured annually at the Kentucky Women Writers Conference. Having lived most of her life in Kentucky, Bianca's poems reflect the trials and triumphs of growing up as a woman of color in a border state.

Kelli Stevens Kane is a poet, playwright, and oral historian. Her poetry manuscript, Hallelujah Science, was a Finalist for the 2011 Four Way Books Levis Poetry Prize, and a Semifinalist for the Persea Books 2011 Lexi Rudnitsky First Book Prize in Poetry. She's a 2011 August Wilson Center Fellow, a 2011 Cave Canem Fellow, a 2011 Flight School Fellow, and the recipient of a 2011 Advancing Black Arts in Pittsburgh Grant. (kellistevenskane.com)

Matthew Stranach is from a small town in Atlantic Canada. He is currently living overseas. He is also a proud dad.

Michelle Whittaker is a poet and pianist. Her research interest includes eco-poetics and creative non-fiction. Her poems have recently appeared and are forthcoming in The New Yorker, The Southampton Review, Xanadu, Drunken Boat, and Long Island Quarterly. She has received the 2009 Jody Donohue Poetry Prize, a Pushcart Prize honorable mention, and a Cave Canem fellowship. The Floater was first published online in Lemon Hound. Stones Formerly Known As Love was first published in The Southhampton Review.

Donna Williams has nurtured a hobby, then a career as a British Sign Language Poet. She participated in the Metaphor in Creative Sign Language Project, run by Dr. Rachel Sutton-Spence of Bristol University, a project to encourage, study, and permanently record poetry performed in Sign Language. The project has since concluded, but Donna continues to develop her poetry with interest in bi-lingual poetry, whether in the form of translating English poems (her own or other poets') into BSL or through English voiceovers for her BSL poems. She works with BSL interpreters to produce and perform bi-lingual poetry and also performs collaboratively with other poets. This anthology is her third English poetry publication. Many of her poems, whether English or BSL, reference and reflect her identity as a deaf LGBT sign-language-using poet, using both serious and comedic themes.

Phillip B. Williams is a Chicago, Illinois native and a Cave Canem fellow. His work is published or is forthcoming in Callalo, Sou'wester, Painted Bride Quarterly, Gertrude and others. He is currently the Poetry Editor of the online literary journal, Vinyl Poetry and an HIV Tester and Prevention Counselor for Chicago House and Social Services through AIDS United's AmeriCorps program. His chapbook, Bruised Gospels was released by Bloom Books in 2011.

Keith Wilson is an Affrilachian Poet and editor for the multi-lingual online journal Public-Republic. Some of his recent publications include Appalachian Heritage, The Dead Mule School of Southern Literature, Mobius: The Journal of Social Change, Evergreen Review, and Breadcrumb Scabs. Keith currently lives in Northern Kentucky.

L. Lamar Wilson's poems have appeared in African American Review, Callaloo, jubilat, Los Angeles Review, The 100 Best African American Poems, and other journals and anthologies. His poetry collection, Sacrilegion, is the winner of the Carolina Wren Press Poetry Series (2013). He's received fellowships from the Cave Canem Foundation, the Alfred E. Knobler

Scholarship Fund, and the Arts and Sciences Foundation at the University of North Carolina at Chapel Hill, where he is a doctoral candidate in African American and multi-ethnic poetics.

Renee Zepeda is currently living in the Pocono Mountains of Pennsylvania. Her work in The White Space Poetry Anthology first appeared in her collaborative double book, The Twitstat Project (with Chris Weige). She is currently at work on a novel of future fiction called Boy Energy: Notes on Departure. Her magazine, The PR, exists online: scribd.com/renee_zepeda and thepr.tumblr.com. Follow her on Twitter: twitter.com/ThePR

THE EDITOR

Maya Washington has a BA in Theatre from the University of Southern California and an MFA in Creative Writing from Hamline University. Her work is featured in The Playwrights' Center Monologues for Women (Heinemann Drama, 2005). Her one-act, Colorful Women of Invention, was produced at Youth Performance Company in 2003. Her poem, "January First", is featured in the Family Housing Fund's Home Sweet Home Again touring exhibition. Her full-length play South of Adams, West of Figueroa was selected as a participant in Congo Square Theatre's August Wilson Playwriting Initiative in 2008. A proud Cave Canem Graduate Fellow, her work has also appeared in international literaray journals. She recently produced, wrote and directed the award-winning short film, White Space, in addition to editing this companion collection, The White Space Poetry Anthology. Maya Washington is the Creative Director of Running Water Entertainment, LLC and White Space Poetry Project.

WHITE SPACE POETRY PROJECT

White Space Poetry Project began in the Spring of 2010 in response to the minimal exposure of deaf artists, specifically poets, within the mainstream world of film and literary arts. Historically, deaf artists' voices have been absent from the larger mainstream conversations within the worlds of independent film and poetry. While a thriving arts community exists within the Deaf World, the average hearing audience member has not been exposed to the scope or vibrant diversity of the work of deaf artists unless they have a personal tie (family member or friend) to the Deaf Community. Our mission is rooted in illuminating the poetry, ideas, and performance of talented artists throughout the world by suggesting that deaf and hearing artists can commingle on the page, stage, and big screen. White Space Poetry Project is fiscally sponsored by Fractured Atlas, an arts service organization. It is a pilot endeavor of Running Water Entertainment, LLC a creative media production company.

Marisa Quinn

33498693R00073

Made in the USA
Charleston, SC
17 September 2014